THE AUTHC

Tim Bowden is a broadcaster, radio and television documentary maker, historian and author. He has worked as a foreign correspondent in Asia (covering the Vietnam war) and in North America. In 1969 he was the first executive producer of the ABC radio current affairs program *PM*, before becoming a producer with the ground-breaking television current affairs program *This Day Tonight* in the early 1970s. For the last 30 years Tim Bowden has been actively broadcasting, writing and researching Australian activities in Antarctica, He has written the official history of ANARE Australian National Antarctic Research Expeditions) *The Silence Calling - Australians in Antarctica 1947-97*, published in June, 1997. He also presented six half-hour documentaries *Breaking The Ice* on ABC-TV in 1996. Tim received an Order of Australia for services to public broadcasting in June 1994. In May 1997 he was awarded an honorary degree of Doctor of Letters from the University of Tasmania. He now lives in the Wilds of Tuncurry.

Rod Ledingham was raised in Scotland and first worked in the Antarctic in 1966 as a meteorologist for the British Antarctic Survey. He over-wintered in 1967 and 1968 at Adelaide Island (near Rothera Base) and Fossil Bluff. Returning briefly to the UK he moved to Australia in 1970, working as a geologist for six years before again returning to the sub-antarctic with his wife Jeannie. They wintered twice on Macquarie Island in 1977 and 1980, and spent a summer at the site of Mawson's Australasian Antarctic Expedition Hut at Commonwealth Bay in 1978. In 1980 Rod commenced work as field equipment and training officer with the Australian Antarctic Division and remained there until 2003 equipping, training, and running field expeditions and re-supply ships to the Australian sector stations Casey, Davis and Mawson and several summer bases. Rod began escorting tourist voyages in 1991 and has visited Antarctica most seasons since 1976, mainly to the Ross Sea but also to the Peninsula.

Other Books by Tim Bowden from ETT IMPRINT

Ion Idriess: The Last Interview

No Plucking!

Ross Bowden: Trailblazer

One Crowded Hour (audio)

ABANDONED AT FOSSIL BLUFF

Antarctic Peninsula

By Tim Bowden and Rod Ledingham

This 2nd edition published by ETT Imprint, Exile Bay 2022

ETT IMPRINT
PO Box R1906
Royal Exchange NSW 1225 Australia

First published by Pheonix Design in 2016.
First electronic edition published by ETT Imprint in 2022

ISBN   978-1-922698-72-8   (pbk)
ISBN   978-1-922698-73-5   (ebk)

Cover: The Fearless Five waiting for winter.
From left: Martyn Bramwell, Col the dog. Graham Smith.
Front: John Walsh. Seated: John Ayres, Rod Ledingham.

CHAPTERS

••••••••

PROLOGUE

In January 1995 I travelled to the Ross Sea on the *Kapitan Khlebnikov* a Russian icebreaker chartered by the travel adventure company Adventure Associates. One of my co-lecturers on this voyage was Rod Ledingham, resident of Oyster Cove near Kettering, Tasmania, an experienced Antarctic veteran whom I first knew through his field work with the Australian Antarctic Division, but as I was about to discover, had cut his Antarctic teeth with the British Antarctic Survey (BAS) in the late 1960s. He gave a wonderful illustrated lecture on a particular incident that took place in the summer of 1967-68 when he was assisting a geologist mapping high on the Antarctic plateau, driving a sledge dog team. He had been flown in by a light aircraft to take over the other dog team, but after their field work had ended, the aircraft crashed on take-off, fortunately with no casualties to the men or dogs. With no replacement aircraft available, and communications basic to say the least, the pilot and his two passengers had to use the sledge dogs to sledge 200 km along the plateau and down a glacier which had only been travelled once before to a small hut at Fossil Bluff on the coast, where two other BAS personnel were waiting to be flown out. So began a year of basic survival, with five men in a hut designed for four, minimal fuel for heating, no extra clothing and barely enough food.

Recalling Rod's extraordinary lecture, I asked him a few years ago if he had a video of it. He did not! A former passenger on a later voyage did have one, but sadly died before he could send it. I determined that this story should be told, and began from scratch, interviewing Rod Ledingham about those events, knowing that there were many excellent photographs to support the narrative.

****

CHAPTER ONE

The Crash

In the summer of 1967-68 Rod Ledingham, then 23-years-old in his second year of service with the British Antarctic Survey on the Antarctic Peninsula. As a meteorologist, he did not expect to be some 2000 metres up among the peaks and glaciers of the Antarctica plateau, driving a dog team with one of the BAS geologists Graham Smith. He had been at Fossil Bluff for a month while it was being resupplied for the summer season program the next year. Graham's previous field assistant Lew Wylie had fallen and hit his head on a rock, and had to be evacuated to the main base, Stonington, in Marguerite Bay in western Graham Land. Ledingham was flown in to replace him and drive his dog team, the 'Admirals'. (For safety in crevassed country teams always travelled in pairs.)

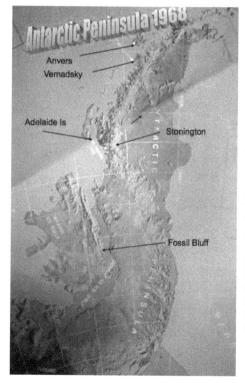

In the 1960s, the British Antarctic Service still operated in a way with which the ill-fated polar explorer Robert Falcon Scott would have been familiar. Fieldwork was done with wooden sledges pulled by husky dogs, which carried tents and supplies. The accommodation at Fossil Bluff was basic – four bunks in a hut built on a rocky scree overlooking George VI Sound. This was a men-only operation. Women were not permitted to winter with BAS until early 1996.

Fossil Bluff was only occupied in the short summer season from October to March, refuelling aircraft from a basic skiway marked out with oil drums south of the hut.

A typical field camp high on the plateau, with a polar pyramid tent for two men, and a dog sledge with a wheel to measure distance.

A standard dog team was usually seven to nine dogs, seen here pulling a sledge on the sea ice.

Towards the end of February radio instructions came in for Ledingham and Smith to depot their equipment and remaining supplies on a *nunatak* (a rock protruding from the ice cap) ready for next season's mapping, and prepare to be picked up by a Pilatus Porter aircraft, piloted by John Ayres. The eight dogs had to come out on the same flight.

The aircraft landed on the ice safely, and while Smith sat beside the pilot in the front cockpit, Ledingham had the less enviable job of climbing into the cargo space with the dogs.

The versatile Pilatus Porter after landing on the ice high on the Plateau.

'I had to lie in the back, on the floor with the dogs and try to keep them apart. The procedure was that as soon as we got airborne, the aircraft's heater was turned up full blast, and they go to sleep almost instantly. It's quite amazing.' The dogs didn't like the jolting over the *sastrugi* ice-field, but worse was to come.

'As we were taking off and just about to become airborne, there was a BANG and we shot around in a big circle and broke off the main right-hand ski.

'A dogfight immediately broke out in the cabin and eventually I calmed them down after a lot of kicking and punching. Then I looked out the window and saw the tail wheel and the ski lying outside on the ice. The accident had also torn the whole rudder post off the back of the aircraft.'

The Pilatus Porter had ground-looped when the take-off failed (see the trench in the snow gouged by the broken tail wheel and rudder-post).

They immediately realised the precariousness of their situation, because three weeks before, the only other aircraft in the area, a single radial-engined Otter, had broken down taking off from Stonington, when the engine cut out, and the aircraft crash landed on the ice.

The three men and eight dogs waited for a few days, until the pilot, John Ayres, suggested he try and take off in the crippled aircraft. He proposed they took the other ski off. Ayers said, 'I'll try and take off when the wind gets up – I can lift the tail off using prop wash and take off into the wind and I can be airborne without any more damage'. Rod Ledingham knew that the empty aircraft could often get airborne in about 20 or 30 metres against a strong wind. In the meantime they took off the left-hand ski to balance things up. After another two days they got a suitable wind of 20 to 30 knots, and they pulled the Pilatus Porter round on its belly to face into the wind. They took the medical kit out and buried it in the ice, just in case it was needed in a hurry.

John Ayers ruefully inspects the broken off ski and rudder post.

'So John tried to take off but just as he was about to lift off, a wheel dug into the hard plateau snow and the aircraft went up on its nose. Its tail went right up in the air, and crashed back and bent all the rear end. The prop hit the snow and was badly bent. We saw grey smoke and thought there might be fire, so we ran up to the plane and wrenched the door open and pulled John out. He was OK fortunately. But the gas turbine stopping dead from 30 000 rpm is not good for it. The cloud of grey smoke cleared – we presumed it was unburned fuel.

The Pilatus Porter, stripped of its skis, waits for a suitably strong wind to attempt a take-off.

'In retrospect it was probably a good thing that he crashed on the plateau, because if had he made it back to Adelaide Island at sea level, the snow would have been very soft for a wheeled landing and may well have caused a much worse accident.'

A forlorn sight, the Pilatus Porter its bent propellers signalling that it would definitely never fly again!

With the aircraft now finally out of action, they decided to take the shortest route down to Fossil Bluff, but there were some big crevassed glaciers to negotiate. While they still had battery life in the Pilatus Porter and a working radio, Ledingham talked with an experienced sledging hand, Geordie MacLeod, at Stonington who had been down the route they intended to take, and he described roughly how they should tackle the big glacier that ran down to King George VI Sound, in the Batterbee Mountains.

Smith and Ledingham were experienced sledgers, but the pilot, John Ayres, was a complete novice. Ledingham:

'We had eight dogs, so we planned to split them into two teams of four. Graham would go ahead one day, and I'd do the next, and so on. The pilot, John Ayers would travel behind the back sledge as the safest option.'

At least they all had skis, which were safer in crevassed country. As Rod Ledingham explained, 'The dogs would punch holes through the snow with their feet quicker than a sledge would, and you were on skis behind the whole lot.

'You always wore a harness around your waist and a loop about half-a-metre long, which you put on the handlebars of the sledge. If you fell through a crevasse, you would be pulled out of it by the sledge. And if the sledge and dogs all vanished down a crevasse, you would hopefully lift off the loop before you went in as well. That was the idea anyway.'

****

CHAPTER TWO

Dash To The Coast

There were two options for the stranded field party, with no aircraft available anywhere on the Peninsula to come to their rescue: to sledge to the main British Antarctic Survey (BAS) at Stonington, near Adelaide island, 400 kilometres to the north, or take the shorter journey to the Fossil Bluff hut.

Porter Nunatak was named after the crash site. The shorter journey to Fossil Bluff was preferred to the longer and more hazardous route to Stonington.

The longer journey was by far the more hazardous, as Rod Ledingham has since seen maps of the terrain in later years which was criss-crossed by numerous glaciers along the way. But there was another urgent reason why the shorter journey 210 km route south-west to Fossil Bluff needed to be taken. Ledingham knew that there were two young men who had recently been dropped off by BAS at the Fossil Bluff hut and who had expected to be flown back to Adelaide Island (with Ledingham's marooned field party) in the Pilatus Porter aircraft. They were novices, with no Antarctic experience whatsoever, so Ledingham thought it best if they went down and joined them and looked after them through what was going to be an unscheduled wintering at Fossil Bluff.

The two sledges were packed with equipment and provisions, with four dogs to each sledge – well short of a conventional husky team of at least nine. Taking a last mournful glance at their once-proud red Pilatus Porter, with snowdrifts already building up around it, they began their descent from the polar plateau. Crevasses were the greatest hazard, even while still high on the plateau.

Smith's team was leading, with Ledingham following, and the pilot John Ayres skiing alongside the second sledge.

Rod Ledingham: 'Graham stopped a few days later and walked back to me to discuss the route, and plopped into a crevasse running diagonally across the front of my sledge – I flicked him my ski tow, and he popped out like a cork from a bottle. A few days later, with very few incidents, we had crossed the Millet, Bertram and Ryder Glaciers each about 15 to 30 kilometres wide, and began our descent through the Batterbee Mountains high up on the plateau, down on to the Otter Glacier.

'I nearly drove over a big cliff into a huge crevasse near the top of the glacier – which Graham later named "Ledingham's Leap". Fortunately the dogs stopped and were looking back at me. I was wondering why they had halted and wandered down to the front – having tied myself to the centre trace – to find they were looking at a bloody great hole in front of us. So it was just as well they stopped!'

The journey south begins across the upper Millet, Bertram and Ryder Glaciers. With only four dogs per team they made remarkably good time, but there were hidden hazards.

The really tricky part of the journey was the Otter Glacier that ran right down to King George VI Sound. The start point was Mount Cadbury (2000 m). The glacier flowed west some 50km down a steep valley on the south side of the Batterbee Mountains.

Before they left, they were lucky to be able to talk on the radio to experienced sledging hand, Geordie MacLeod, who had been down that route, and he advised travelling on the right hand northern side of the glacier.

Rod Ledingham in radio contact with Stoningon Base on their dash to the coast.

Both Ledingham and the pilot John Ayres reminded Smith that they remembered hearing Geordie MacLeod, the man who had actually been down the same route, and who had recommended the north side of the glacier during the radio sked, as it was badly crevassed on the south side. But Smith, who was the most experienced sledger said, 'No, it was the south side.' Ledingham figured it was his sledge party they had joined after all. Smith got his way, and the party were soon tackling 'monster crevasses', which Ledingham said were 'just a nightmare. We couldn't cross these things so had to retrace our steps and zig-zag our way back up and it was very dodgy.'

The second dog team would see the lead team nearby and try to cut the corners, as if to say, 'To hell with going the long way round'. Rod Ledingham recalled, 'It was difficult to get the following team to stop cutting corners, and there were several hairy leaps across quite big crevasses. They were 10 to 15 metres in the widest bits.'

Eventually it was agreed to take MacLeod's advice, and they moved over to the northern side of the glacier.

'We still found lots of crevasses, but we were going so fast that we were actually leaping across them. The dogs would occasionally fall in and would be plucked out by the other huskies in this mad rush down that bloody glacier. It was exhilarating but terrifying just the same – one mad hurtle to the safety of the Sound!'

The welcome sight of the sea ice on King George VI Sound near Fossil Bluff

Mercifully they reached the bottom of the glacier without any accidents, and set out the next day over thirty kilometres of flat ice to the hut at Fossil Bluff.

Ledingham admitted they were very relieved to get there. But there was an unexpected surprise. They arrived with eight huskies, only to find there was a total of ten! The lead bitch gave birth to two pups the day after they arrived.

The two young men, now also marooned at the Fossil Bluff hut, were exceedingly relieved to see them. They were John Walsh, an aircraft mechanic, and Martyn Bramwell – like Rod Ledingham – a meteorological observer.

The hut at Fossil Bluff was for summer parties only and not designed for winter occupation. For example there was no 'cold porch', a small area separating the interior of the hut from the outside door, insulating the warmer interior from the below zero blasts of cold air that would otherwise have come straight in – as they later did. In hindsight, Ledingham said, they should have built one, but by the time winter came, it was too late and they didn't have the materials to do so anyway.

The Fossil Bluff Hut – designed for four people, with five about to winter in it. The coal bags stacked between the hut and the weather instrument box were not enough for heating – just for cooking. Note the dog sledges stacked on the roof.

Because BAS had been flying in provisions for the following year's season, there was enough food – and dog food – to last the five men for a year. But keeping warm would be their biggest challenge, as the Aga cooker used coal, and there were only 60 bags – 27 kilos each – which meant there were only four-and-a-half to seven kilos of coal per day which meant they could only use the stove for cooking in the evenings and not for general heating.

There were also only four bunks for five men. But there was a spare camp stretcher, fortunately. Someone had to sleep in the camp bed, on the floor of the hut. What heat there was in the hut rose (as heat does) to the ceiling of the hut. The coldest spot in the hut was the camp bed, and the lower bunks were colder than the upper ones. A roster was drawn up with a five-week cycle. Ledingham:

'I would sleep on the floor for a week then move to the lower left hand bunk. The person there would move to the floor, then to the upper bunks, so everyone had a week on the floor every 5th week. When it started to get colder (the floor was – 20 degrees Centigrade at times) and for the bottom bunk you had to have a full sleeping bag when you went to bed.'

'In a top bunk you'd only need a sheet bag when you went to sleep, because the air in the hut was so layered, and as the night went on you'd get into a part of the sleeping bag, and that would be enough. But on the floor you'd have to have a double bag, so there were all these complex combinations for the sleeping bags.'

The Fearless Five waiting for winter. From left: Martyn Bramwell, Col the dog. Graham Smith. Front: John Walsh. Seated: John Ayres, Rod Ledingham.

Just how cold it was on the floor was revealed during the winter when Rod Ledingham was looking under a bunk for something, and found a pair of boots which were totally encased in an block of ice, which had crept in under the walls!

Unexpected arrivals: Mother Nova and one of her pups Pung

Three months later – the growing Chow and Pung

Because Ledingham had been appointed the Base Commander for Adelaide Island for the coming season, he was instructed by radio to take charge of the enforced wintering party at Fossil Bluff. Managing personal relations in such a confined and crowded space was tricky at times but on the whole they were a happy crew with lots of joking and tomfoolery.

Ledingham: 'It was good at the start, and all of us got on pretty well. Graham, the geologist, was usually chirpy and quick witted, but could be a bit firey at times. I shouldn't say that really but he could be a bit fiery. John Walsh and Martyn Bramwell were genial and easy going. The odd man out was the pilot, John Ayers. He was the oldest in the hut, in his forties, while the rest of us were in our early twenties.

'He wasn't going to be very popular anyway, because when he flew to Fossil Bluff from Adelaide Island he didn't tell anyone. He was supposed to bring eggs, and the mail and all sorts of stuff that we were looking forward too, but he just forgot. John was also a bit humourless. His sole enthusiasms were radios and aircraft. He was always ready to divert any conversation about women, skiing or fast cars – or anything really – and then change it to, say, aircraft. But then he had been flying for many years and was a very accomplished pilot – British aerobatics champion no less.'

Rod Ledingham described the hut at Fossil Bluff as small and basic. 'We had a barometer there, met screen, a wind speed indicator and a whole bunch of radios, only one of which actually worked, but we left them there because they looked good in photos. One was from Sir Vivian Fuchs' Trans Antarctic Expedition in 1957-58, and it had a plaque on it saying "detonator". Apparently they used it to fire shots when they were doing seismic surveys during the crossing. The only one that worked was just a portable military radio, and we added the one we carried with the dogs – it was very good actually. We would pass weather every day to Adelaide Island and Stonington Base for the aircraft.'

As the long winter in Fossil Bluff hut began, the four younger men got on well, and as they were Goon Show fans, that zany humour became a part of hut badinage. The outsider was the older man, pilot John Ayers, who had no great sense of humour or at least it was different to the rest of the party. To give him his due he had not been designated to spend a second year down south.

As the winter progressed, Rod Ledingham decided to take Ayres away from the hut on field trips man-hauling a dog sled, 'to give the others a bit of a break', and do some glaciological work.

'We used to play Mah Jong every night pretty well, and other card games. The cooking was on a two days roster. You did two days, and then two days as 'gashie', washing up and clearing away. I used to follow Graham Smith. That was a lot of work, because he used to dirty every pot and pan in the bloody hut. We only had one washing bowl, and that was also used for brewing.

'We did the brewing in the rafters and mixed any concoction we could dream up – we'd heard that raisins and sultanas would produce yeast, so we'd use these to start fermentation, and we'd put in anything sugary, like jam. After a couple of days we'd drink the brew, and get quite merry. A doctor at Stonington did say such a brew would produce nasty side effects – I think he called them esters – which was probably poisoning us to some extent. Anyway we had some fun doing that.'

Most of the hut's crew – except John Ayers – tried their best to make their cooking interesting, trying their hands at biscuits or fancy food like profiteroles. They baked bread every two days, because there was enough flour in their supplies to sustain that. One of Rod Ledingham's specialities was a non-lumpy custard. Martyn Bramwell was a crusty pastry specialist. And there were experiments. Ledingham:

'One was a kind of dumpling thing that I made once. The only dish towel that we had was very grey, I remember that much. I boiled up this dough of dried apricots and sweetened dough and put it in our only dish towel, knotted it and tied it up tight and boiled it in a pot. When it came out and you peeled back the dish-towel there was this thing that looked like a foetus, slightly grey, ingrained with dirt from the dish towel. It tasted quite nice actually but it looked bloody horrible when you got it out – a watery, anaemic looking thing, like a boiled baby.

'No one looked forward to John Ayres' cooking – his slack approach was to take two tins of tomatoes, chuck them in a pan and put in two tins of chopped up tongue. We didn't particularly like tongue, I don't know why. On principle we'd always give him a hard time every time he produced it – he cooked it every time because it was easy. We called it "boiled afterbirth", and he said, "Look, if you don't like boiled afterbirth then just tell me". And we said, "We don't like boiled afterbirth".

'To reinforced the message, we buried the tins of tongue up on a hillside in a pit in the snow so he couldn't make it any more.'

****

CHAPTER THREE

Learning To Be A 'Gashie'

As a schoolboy in Inverness, Rod Ledingham joined his school climbing club, so beginning a life-long fascination with adventuring in wild and remote places. At 18, he began to study geography at Aberdeen University and saw an advertisement in the Geography Department offering a position in the British Antarctic Survey. He immediately applied, and was interviewed by a noted Antarctic explorer and glaciologist, Dr Charles Swithinbank – who 'told me to come back when I was bigger' – after he had completed his degree in geography, with an emphasis on glacial geomorphology in the Scottish Highlands.

The next time he was successful, not as glaciologist, but as a meteorology observer and later as a field assistant and dog driver to the scientists working with the British Antarctic Survey. Field assistants were called 'gash hands ' and were generally very experienced mountaineers or had been in Antarctica in some cases many times. General Assistants ensured the safety of the scientist and took over work to give the scientists time to write up the results of their research To prepare for Antarctic service, Ledingham, in company with a 'pretty polyglot bunch' were sent to the Admiralty in London for eight weeks to study meteorology.

I seem to remember that we spent a lot of time tracking pilot balloons. A met. theodolite has a right angle bend so you can look into the end, and look upwards to track a balloon. But it also meant that if you were tracking a person, you were facing a different direction. So we used to spend a lot time tracking the attractive young secretaries at the Admiralty at lunchtime, and I remember we used to shout bearings and co-ordinates to each other if we saw anything interesting.'

Rod Ledingham, Trainee 'Gashie' at 23

This was followed by five weeks in northern Scotland at RAF Kinloss, at a regular Met Office, spending a lot of time studying how forecasts were made for the Shackleton aircraft stationed there.

Sir Raymond Priestly in his 80s

Eventually the students attended a weekend conference in Cambridge on the British Antarctic scientific programs, where, on the last talk of the whole week, they were lectured to by Sir Raymond Priestley, then in his early eighties.

'We thought, "Oh, he's going to be a really boring old guy" and debated whether to sneak off to the pub or not, but we thought they might do a headcount or something. So we went to the lecture and it was absolutely superb – indeed inspirational – and stood me in good stead later as events turned out.'

[Sir Raymond Priestley talked about how Scott's Northern Party (of which he had been a member) had been collected from Cape Adare and in January 1912, were dropped off at Inaccessible Island for a few weeks, while the ship picked up the main party at Cape Evans. But the ship was unable to penetrate the ice to return, and they were left to winter in a snow cave. Eventually in the spring they made their way along the coast to Cape Evans. They had six weeks rations for seven months, plus whatever seals and penguins they could kill. They were picked up by expedition ship *Terra Nova* a year later. Captain Scott's South Pole Party had all died during the Northern Party's own ordeal. Priestley's lecture was recalled in 1966-67 when Rod Ledingham faced his own survival experience at Fossil Bluff.]

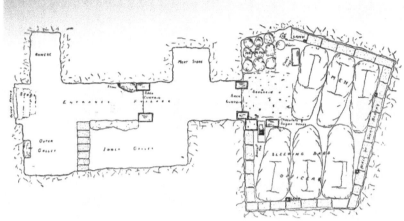

PLAN OF IGLOO.

A drawing of the ice cave, tunnelled into the side of a hill, at Inexpressible Island where Priestley's party of six men spent an enforced winter when the expedition ship Terra Nova was unable to pick them up after their summer sledging exploration on the coast north of Cape Adare, in 1912. Even in these dire conditions, the sleeping chamber carefully separated the three officers from the three other ranks!

This blurred photograph shows the door to the underground cavern where the six stranded members of Scott's Northern Party were forced to winter, subsisting mostly on seal meat with seal blubber lamps for lighting. The only variation to this diet was the occasional Emperor penguin that could be shot. Rod Ledingham's later forced wintering at Fossil Bluff was four-star by comparison.

A few months later, Ledingham was based at Adelaide Island Base T, on the south west coast of Graham Land, where they had 40 dogs.

Ledingham: 'Dogs and light aircraft were the mainstay of the whole BAS operation exploring, mapping and doing geology in southern Grahamland. Stonington had about five or six field parties out, which meant they had a scientist and a field assistant, generally someone who was very experienced in the field, a mountaineer and had already done a winter or two, and over 100 dogs. The scientists were geologists, geophysicists and a surveyors.'

The dogs were flown into the field in a new Pilatus Porter and the single-engined Otter aircraft. Ledingham said the Porter was about the size of a small station waggon. 'Our job was to train the pups and take them out to the field when dogs were needed to keep up numbers in the teams and to lay depots and collect samples from the field parties.

Loading huskies into the Pilatus Porter on Adelaide Island for distant field trips

A dog training run in summer on Adelaide Island

'We tied the dogs against the sides of the cargo space. It is pretty tiny, and sometimes you would have eight or nine large dogs roughly the size of Alsatians, plus we only had one spare seat. So sometimes when we had two people flying, one had to lie down in the middle and help to separate the dogs, and keep the peace.'

The dog teams were scattered all over the southern peninsula of Grahamland on various scientific projects, including mapping, geology, gravity surveys and most working high on the plateau at an altitude of roughly 2000 metres. Ledingham:

'One of our tasks was to resupply Fossil Bluff a field hut 240 nautical miles to the south on Alexander Island. So we'd hop in with the pilot on a really good day then the pilot would fly maybe three times to Fossil Bluff which is about a two to two-and-a-half hour flight. The passenger in the front seat could take over in the Otter if the pilot needed a rest – you pulled out a pin on the yoke and you could pivot the steering column across to the other person who was with you. You'd push the pin back and lock it and then you could steer, and the pilot could have a nap. You didn't go if you couldn't see where you were going basically. It was just a matter of driving down across Marguerite Bay down to the King George VI Sound.

'It took a while to get the hang of going straight and maintaining altitude and direction. So we'd fly along and then when the pilot had a bit of a snooze and when we got near Fossil Bluff, we'd wake him up and say, "Hey, you can have it back now and land it".'

*The main British Antarctic Survey
base on the Antarctic Peninsula*

Rod Ledingham spent his first winter from 1966-67 at Adelaide Island. Then in the following summer, he was sent to Fossil Bluff, 'just to stay for a month' to man the radio and pass weather information back to base so they could keep sending the supplies down.

'After a short while they said, "Rod, we want you to go up on the plateau and take over a dog team for Graham Smith – a geologist there doing mapping the Grahamland plateau – and whose field assistant has fallen down a steep slope and banged his head, and was concussed".'

The rest, as they say, is history. Ledingham did not stay at Fossil Bluff for a month, but almost an entire year – from 15 January 1967 to 21 December 1968.

****

CHAPTER FOUR

Life In The Hut

The Fossil Bluff hut with Mt Pyramid in the background

The Fossil Bluff routine was two days cooking followed by two days 'gashie' – cleaning up – and six days off. Four of the five did meteorological observations to be radioed to the main Stonington base, and then to London, after Rod Ledingham and Martyn Bramwell taught the others how to do them.

The radio and meteorological desk in the crowded little hut

The usual routine for a well-staffed operation was to take the weather readings every three hours. But the main burden fell on the qualified met observers, Ledingham and Bramwell, who decided to tell London that they couldn't do the night observations because of opening the door in the middle of the night. As Fossil Bluff was a summer station, there was no cold porch as an airlock and with outside temperatures of –50 degrees C, and no heating possible after dinner, they needed to conserve what heat there was inside. The Fossil Bluff hut was 100 nautical miles from the open sea. Observations were done until midnight and then no more until 9 am, dispensing with the 3 am and 6 am readings. What heat remained in the hut after the evening meal had to be preserved.

In the Fossil Bluff hut the five men became used to the routine of juggling the two upper and lower bunks while one person in turn slept on the camp stretcher on the floor, the coldest bed by far. Ledingham recalled the bunks were adorned with photos of the famous fashion model Jean Shrimpton. At the main Adelaide Island base, someone named a dog "Shrimpy". Ledingham:

'She sent some publicity photographs to Antarctica that we drooled over. They were of Jean Shrimpton in a mini skirt. I think she helped to start that fashion, it caused an uproar in UK anyway when they came in, much to our delight, when we got back.'

The four bunks were rotated between the five men. The top bunks were the warmest with the short straw (and coldest) on the camp stretcher on the floor.

With not much to do on days off, there was a lot of extra time for sleeping. The pilot, John Ayres, clocked up 130 hours in one week in bed, making it something of a record. What heat remained in the hut after the evening meal had to be preserved.

In the winter the first meteorological observations were made at 9 am. Rod Ledingham said he went out in his pyjamas, plus fur hat and gloves – especially on Mondays when the thermograph and hydrograph charts had to be changed, and was only out there for a few minutes.

'As you sprinted out the door you could feel your pyjamas stiffen – they froze instantly as you ran to the screen. We'd sprint out, do the obs, work the screen, do the temperatures and anything else at high speed and note the clouds as you came sprinting back. By the time you got inside your clothes were clunking as you walked around. Then you'd stand by the cooker for a while you thawed out as well as your pyjamas, and then you got back into bed. When we left months later there was still a piece of skin from my tongue left on the thermograph drum chart catches from the time I attempted to open them with my teeth'.

Rod Ledingham pouring a brew at the coal-fuelled Aga stove

The coal fire would be fired up in the late afternoon for cooking the evening meal. Breakfast and lunch were cooked on a primus stove. During the winter, lunch was just hot soup and if the cook was feeling generous he would do the midday weather observations as well. To make best use of the heat retained in the hut, they would usually stay up playing cards or Mah Jong until midnight or 1 pm in the morning, then go to bed as the hut started to cool down.

At Fossil Bluff the toilet out the back was just a pyramid tent and by the time the winter came snow had almost completely covered it – leaving just a foot or two visible at the apex. Ledingham:

'We had to crawl down to it. We discovered that the production of turds was actually equal to the consumption of sugar in quantity because every time we filled a bin we had to open another sugar tin. We had a frame and a toilet seat over which you hovered when it was in the minus 30s and 40s Centigrade. The problem was the husky pups used to get in there too and spread their turds all over the place. Then they'd come into the hut and would be licking you. Then you'd go into the dunny and find they'd been in there, and what they did. Dogs quite commonly ate turds after they'd been in the field for a while – their own, and sometimes ours as well.'

The northern tip of the Antarctic Peninsula is the farthest north part of Antarctica, but Alexander Island was 71 degrees south. The sun wasn't seen for about three or four months, but it was never completely pitch black. Of course in a blizzard it was dark, but most nights even with stars out it was quite bright, and with the moon, Ledingham recalled, 'You could even read by its light'.

Rod Ledingham had already experienced one winter at Adelaide Island Base T and had experience of getting on with other expeditioners at close quarters.

The toilet tent. A bracing experience at –40C, with or without the enhancement of husky puppies' turds.

'I often thought when I worked in places like that you need somebody to bear the brunt of all the complaints. I remember the same happening in the bush in Australia when I worked in a mining town. Back on the main base at Adelaide Island there was this Irishman, Eric. We used to call him "Ericus Antarcticus", and I think he thought he should be sewn into his clothes when he got there because he never washed. I was the only one who talked to him and I was quite often given messages. "Tell Eric to get washed we can't stand it any longer." So I'd have to pass this message on.'

In any case, hygiene in the Fossil Bluff hut was extremely difficult. Ledingham:

'I don't recall what others did but on one occasion – much to the disgust of my hut mates in retrospect – I borrowed the washing up bowl which was also used for making bread and brewing. I tried to have a wash in that. It was big enough to get my feet in but only just. I put in hot water and then stood at the workshop end of the hut and took scoops and poured it over me and all it succeeded in doing was forming a sort of glacier where it froze onto the floor, and I really didn't have much of a wash I must admit. So that was about it and I wasn't encouraged by them to use the all-important bowl. It was a bloody good job it didn't split because it was only plastic.'

Conversation in the hut, Ledingham recalls, was mostly about women and what they would all do when they got back home. When they could get outdoors, they devised their own sports.

'I used to give skiing lessons. I skied quite a lot in the Cairngorms in Scotland, and at the time skis had been upgraded from wooden planks with homemade sycamore ski poles, or bamboo ski sticks, to metal ones, and if you were a really good skier you flashed them in the sun so that people would realise you were a gun skier. So I taught the others the art of "sticksmanship" making sure they flashed when you turned. It didn't matter whether you could ski or not, so long as the sticks flashed and you looked stylish. This was for when we were going to Saint Moritz at some future date, to impress the ladies with our brilliance.'

There was no room in the tiny hut to store supplies, which had to be stacked in crates at the back of the hut.

Although there was plenty of food thanks to the hut being resupplied for a program one year ahead, it was limited in variety. Clothing was in short supply, but Ledingham was worse off than the others, because he thought he was only going to Fossil Bluff for a month. Then he was asked to fly up to dog sledge for a week with Graham Smith.

'I thought, "Oh well, there's no point in taking much kit, because you barely change clothing on a sledging party". So I got rid of everything apart from my mukluks and a pair of Argentinian pyjamas, my wind proofs and a Norwegian jersey which I'd already worn for a year or more, and went up to do the dog sledging.

'Of course when I went back to Fossil Bluff there wasn't any clobber there that I could borrow, and so I had to wear this outfit for the next year. First of all I'd darn what I could, then put on patches, then more darns, and then the holes in the darns. Then the patches were patched and darned again, and so on. I finished up replacing my socks with my jersey sleeves. With sea boot stockings, the foot had disintegrated. First I turned the foot the other way round so the heel was on top and then it wore out the other side and then I put them on sideways and patched them with felt. They lasted reasonably well.

'For entertainment we had the *Calling Antarctica* program on BBC with comedians Harry Secombe and Ken Dodd making wonderful jokes about Antarctica, and only about six to ten small vinyl records, with Eartha Kitt being the most popular by far, played on a tiny plastic record player driven by a clutch of "D" cells soldered in series. The correct speed was achieved by moving the two contacts along the cells as close as we could get to the right speed. Sometimes it was perfect for a short while!'

****

CHAPTER FIVE

The Odd Man Out

Fossil Bluff Hut in the grip of winter

With no doctor available, and four A1 fit young men (this is a requirement of Antarctic service with the British Antarctic Survey and the Australian Antarctic Division), most did not dwell on what might happen in the event of serious illness. This did, however, prey on the mind of John Ayres, the oldest of the party, who made the mistake of reading through the one medical book in the limited Fossil Bluff hut library. Rod Ledingham:

'I remember John Ayres coming to me and whispering that he thought he might have gallstones and that he might not survive and that sort of stuff, but nothing eventuated.'

Indeed, the rest of the party took part in extreme sports through boredom, when they could get out of the hut, and with the exuberance of youth did not worry about the consequences. Ledingham said they even set up some quite dangerous ski jumps down the slope behind the hut.

'We took risks no doubt. In fact we got John Ayres to do one. He told us he was a good skier so we enticed him up the slope and said, "Right have a go, show us how to do it because you are such good skier". So we inveigled him up the slope, "A bit higher John, because otherwise you'll go into that dip and you'll slow down too much and fall off the end of the jump".

'Of course you've got to get used to a ski jump. We by that time had mastered the art of crouching as you see champion ski jumpers do, and springing as you go over the edge but John hadn't. In fact he froze in terror as he approached the ramp and went straight up and he stalled, I don't know how far up, but it was a long way up and came down backwards into the slope with a crash, and buried his skis down to the back of his boots and he just lay there groaning. We thought we'd killed him!'

Noctilucent cloud in winter

Ayers was the odd man out in the hut, and he did not help by trying to divert just about every conversation to his own interests of aircraft and radios, while the testosterone-charged younger men's thoughts naturally turned to sex, and fast cars and present girlfriends. That plus his appalling concoctions when his turn came to cook – just chucking a couple of cans into a saucepan and mixing them up – caused tensions in the hut. Ledingham decided he had to get Ayers out of the hut for a while when the tensions became close to boiling point, and organised a field trip just for this purpose.

'So I organised with Dr Charles Swithinbank, the head of the glaciology section at head office in London, to put a line of drums across the King George VI Sound which ran north-south between Alexander Island and the Peninsula. The shelf ice of the Sound obviously flowed into the sea at the north and into the south and I thought that Fossil Bluff was about halfway along and I was interested in trying to find out which way it flows, north or south and or did it separate somewhere?

'Swithinbank said, "Yes". I don't know whether he really wanted this information or whether he thought it would keep us amused for a bit and so we went with a dog team to position a line of fuel drums across the Sound 40 kilometres out.'

In the meantime Ledingham set off with John Ayres on a man-hauling hike which he quickly realised was too ambitious, because they took 280 kilos of food and equipment and it was in the middle of winter and extremely cold.

Some pressure ridges on the edge of King George VI Sound

'It was my first experience of the amount of ice you can generate if you sweat a lot, and another foolish thing I did in those days was to tuck my trousers into my boots because it looked better in the rugged photos – you know big white boots and that sort of stuff. So the first night after hauling for five or six hours in soft snow, which at low temperatures is as slippery as sand, we were still only about four miles from the hut – in fact we could see the guys outside the hut wandering around and hear the dogs barking.

'We got into the tent with the outside temperature around − 30 C. I lit the primus and started to prepare to cook our dinner, when I felt a trickle down my neck. I thought, "What the bloody hell is that", and I pulled my parka off and this great shower of slush went all over the tent. And when I pulled my trousers down, out of each trouser leg slid a big snowball of giant ice crystals, because you're sweating like hell and the ice rattles down your trouser legs and can't escape. So I ended up with this doughnut of snow around the bottom of each leg because I had them tucked into my boots.

'It would have been extremely dangerous if we hadn't had the heater. When the primus is on and you hang your gear up in the tent it's dry within an hour no matter how wet it is. If you take the air, which is −30 C outside, and you put on your primus and your Tilley lamp and you heat it up to 20 degrees, up near the top of the tent it rips moisture out of the clothing and dries it very quickly. I soon learnt to leave my jacket and trouser legs loose so all this ice would fall out. Two days after we left, the hut dwellers followed us out into the Sound, and with the dogs, caught up with us in less than an hour!'

Inside a field tent. Pilot John Ayers (left) out on some R & R (on behalf of the three others in the hut) with the obliging Rod Ledingham.

This was a preliminary run for a number of other excursions, culminating in a major journey in the spring when we were asked to organise a tractor train trip down to the south to lay food and fuel depots for the following season.

Radio communication were essential for safety during field trips, and in general terms, for keeping in communications with Stonington on Adelaide Island, and indeed the main BAS headquarters in the Falkland Islands, at Stanley. By this time the two pups that had been born on the day Ledingham, Smith and Ayers had arrived at Fossil Bluff after escaping from their crashed aircraft, were named Pung and Chow. They had to be given registration numbers by BAS headquarters, and were listed as, 'Two dogs, male'.

'Anyway about a month later we were playing with them in the hut and somebody said, "There's some things missing on these dogs, their balls haven't dropped yet". Of course there was an inspection and we discovered they were both bitches, so we then had to tell BAS Headquarters in Stanley over the radio that we had two bitches and could they change the gender on the registration. Bases all over the Peninsula and even the Amundsen-Scott United States South Pole station chimed in offering useful advice on recognition of the different sexes which was very much appreciated of course!'

To conserve food supplies in the hut, the Fossil Bluffers used to dog sled down the Sound to find previously laid food depots for men and dogs, and eat them.

Considerable ingenuity had to be used to stay on the air. The all-important radio batteries were charged by a small diesel Petter 1.5 kva generator. There was some diesel at Fossil Bluff but in winter, Ledingham said, it looked like pale yellow pea soup.

'On one occasion when John Walsh the engineer was away from the Fossil Bluff hut with a dog team, Ledingham realised that the generator was losing compression almost entirely – in fact it wasn't possible to feel any compression stroke when the starter handle was turned. If it could not be fixed, there could be no more field work – or indeed communications with the outside world.'

Rod Ledingham decided on a technical gamble.

'I took the head off it – but I didn't tell Walshie 'till afterwards, because he knew I was a rank amateur mechanic. Martyn, the met man and I replaced the head gasket with the silver lining of a Weeties packet, put it back on and clamped it all down – and behold it started! We were most impressed at our undoubted skill! The other thing was the one injector. It normally had three holes that squirt the fuel into the combustion chamber. You can test this away from the engine, under pressure, and we found there was only one jet unblocked out of the three, which would have been very poor.

'We spent hours with a piece of stainless steel wire from one of the dog sledge handlebar braces with a match box and fine sandpaper stroking this to whittle it down as thin as a whisker to try and clean the other holes in the injector. Amazingly it worked!'

Even more remarkably, the diesel generator kept on going for the rest of the year. When Ledingham confessed to John Walsh what they had done, he was horrified. If the generator had died, radio communications would have been impossible.

****

CHAPTER SIX

To Be Or Not To Be Rescued

Rod Ledingham combined field training with the new recruits, mechanic John Walsh and Martyn Bramwell, to safeguard their food supplies by locating supply dumps already in existence. One was about 60 kilometres from the hut, and they managed to locate it, in the event of running short of food at Fossil Bluff. It was a standard depot with a drum of fuel, and a pile of dog food and another of man food, and they found it without any trouble.

Towards the end of winter BAS headquarters via Stonington passed on a request to organise a tractor trip 160 kilometres to the south to put in a depot of dog and man food for the field parties to use in the coming summer.

'We jumped at the chance but first of all we had to put the new tracks on a Muskeg tractor – 440 bolts on each one of the tracks in temperatures of –30 C, and each bolt had to be driven through rock-hard rubber. The plan was for the Muskeg to drag a fuel sledge, a cargo sledge with dogs on it and a dog sledge for use when we reached the glaciers further south. It took us a good long time in the winter and Walshie was one of those guys who could actually work with bare hands in –30 C to replace the old tractor tracks.

From left: Rod, Graham and John on the southern Depot laying journey with the Muskeg Tractor

'We went on this journey and we took the dogs with us, and a second sledge. There were two dog sledges on their sides on top of a large cargo sledge that were wrapped in canvas and made into a pen for the dogs. We put the dogs in the back because we figured we'd travel quite fast and Graham and I took it in turns sitting with them and we sledged down to the south end of Adelaide Island towed by the refurbished Muskeg tractor.

'It was a wrestling match for a couple of them on the first day and we had to give them some doses of Largactil – an anti-psychotic medication!'.

Ledingham said that by the second day the dogs loved tractor travel.

The huskies relishing their unaccustomed role as passengers

'They didn't have to run and pull the sledges, and could sit there for hours as though they were at Wimbledon, watching the ice going past. We could see the beautiful cliffs and glaciers of Alexander Island, and then down the Sound to the latitude of Martello Nunatak, at the end of Alexander Island. Doubtless the huskies enjoyed it too.

'So it was quite a fine trip scenically, but then we had endless trouble every night because the blizzards would bury the sledges and the tractor and we'd have to dig them all out and drain the oil from the engine, put it in a can, take it into the tent and boil it on the primus. We had a petrol generator for charging the tractor batteries.

'We'd have to get that going in the tent which would immediately fill with fumes, so we re-discovered a wartime trick of oil dilution. We put several pints of petrol into the engine oil before we shut down the tractor engine while it was still hot. That would loosen up the sump oil so the next time we wanted to start it was nice and sloshy. It would burn off as vapour as the oil heated up.'

Ledingham said that although that sounded dangerous, it was not so in the winter cold. They would also hold a blowlamp on the carburettor float chamber and have another primus stove under the sump. This procedure was also used with radial aircraft engines in the Arctic.

'The petrol would evaporate as the oil heated up. It helped free up the propeller. The oil tended to drain into the bottom cylinder. The propeller had to be turned over by hand before the engine was started. It worked the same way with the tractor engine.

'We would get up at two-hourly intervals through the night and warm the engine up to operating temperature to ensure that it worked in the morning. We had a lot of trouble because it was still very cold in winter with lots of southerly gales and we had hell's own job keeping the tractor going.'

SUCCESS! The Muskeg tractor engine bursts into life for another day's run.

*'This beats workin' – Gerry having
a snooze and ignoring the
spectacular scenery.*

Tractor train on the ice

They ran out of food on the way back, mainly because the last food ration they had with them turned out to be rotten, so had to be dumped. Graham Smith and the dogs went on ahead to get us some food so Ledingham stayed with John Walsh, the mechanic, and they finally got the tractor going after 13 hours of work.

Home away from home

'We returned in thick fog at the end of it all. I walked in front with a compass tied to the tractor with a long rope that Walshie could follow by keeping the windscreen clear with a primus stove in the cab. Some of the fog was caused by the wind blowing our own exhaust fumes from behind the tractor as we travelled north in a southerly gale.'

The Fossil Bluff refugees had hoped to be rescued in September. The first visit from outside would have been the dog teams that were going to come down from Stonington led by an Australian, Alistair McArthur, Base Commander, who was an ex-Papua New Guinea patrol officer. They set off from Stonington to come down to Fossil Bluff in September, but only got about a third to halfway across Marguerite Bay – which is 186 kilometres across – when there was an outbreak of unexpectedly warm weather. Ledingham:

'The ice broke up and they were in dire strife for days, jumping about on ice floes which were breaking up. The weather was vile, the snow soft so they had to throw away everything they carried to the absolute minimum and try and get back to Stonington.

'They floe-hopped all the way back and were very lucky to survive. Two years before that, two dog teams had been out on the ice heading across to the Dion Island Emperor Penguin Rookery, near Adelaide Island, and they vanished! I think nine dogs got back in different places and landed on the coast and were picked up by the Argentinians on one of their bases, San Martine, Debenham Island, near Horseshoe Island. The others were found on Jenny Island, and a few got back to Stonington. But all three men with them all lost their lives.

'That was why Peter Hay, the ship RSS *John Biscoe*'s Third Officer was there staying on at Adelaide Island to fill in a gap the year before I arrived. Our rescue party was very lucky to get out of their predicament and make it back to Stonington alive. That was the end of that attempted rescue. We wept as they threw away all the goodies we had requested and had kindly lumbered themselves with, choccy, tooth-brushes, clothes etc.'

In November the Fossil Bluff party heard the news on the radio sked that BAS had bought a new aircraft that was coming from Canada. It was a Twin Otter – the first one to fly in the Antarctic. It was flown over by a Canadian ferry pilot, with an RAF Squadron Leader, Derek Smith, who was to fly it around the Antarctic Peninsula during the summer. Mike Green was the second pilot for the 'Twotter' – as the the aircraft was immediately nicknamed – and later an additional single-engined Otter was purchased too. They flew in to Deception Island from Canada – first because the British were still there after volcanic activity two years before and the ash runway was still intact.'

They had just had the first of three earthquakes in 1967 and the Chileans had left their base that was badly damaged. It also frightened the hell out of the Argentinians across the bay and they sensibly left their base too.

The British, with traditional stiff upper lips, stayed and suffered the second earthquake that was later, in early1969, but the British runway in was still available at Deception Island at the time the Twin Otter was there in December 1968. Whalers Bay, just inside the entrance to the harbour, a volcanic caldera, eventually became the heated swimming place for thousands of tourists who still visit the devastated island.

Ledingham: 'The aircraft flew down to Adelaide Island in early December. On 10 December it took off from Adelaide Island and it flew down towards us – and got completely lost. I was listening to their radio talk, and let off a pilot balloon to check the local wind and tracked it by theodolite to 3000 metres which we heard was the height they were flying at, best for turbine engines. The wind was 70 knots, a westerly blowing across the Peninsula – a very strong wind. We reported this to Adelaide Island to pass to the aircraft. We had no direct contact with aircraft except via the main bases in those days

'It was cloudy, but we had an open sky in patches above us, so weren't too worried and told them about this strong cross wind. And I don't know whether they ignored it, but anyway they flew down towards us at 3000 metres. Now if they'd stayed at 300 metres they would have been probably below all the weather and they could have come across Marguerite Bay and down the King George VI Sound in safety. The pilot, Derek Smith, apparently said the turbines go better at 3000 metres so they'd fly at that height. So he headed into the cloud.

'There was one radio beacon in the area only and that was at Adelaide Island. It didn't work very well, but some of the time it could be heard up to a 80 kilometre radius. One of the earlier radio operators had actually manufactured it on the base. In those days they had these little crystal things which were two pegs in a wee black box and inside the box was a crystal, a disc of quartz and he'd somehow sanded this down to get it into the frequencies that you use for beacons. And he'd sanded and made it himself and it wasn't very good. The radios weren't very powerful in those days, about 50 watts. It looked impressive in a great big cabinet with lots of knobs, but only marginally better than our field radios. Radio blackouts were common due to solar flares disturbing the ionosphere. That could also be a problem with the direction-finding beacon – in short the beacon was unreliable.'

The Twin Otter pilot, Derek Smith, began to fly down towards Fossil Bluff to pick them up with about five extra people – six in total on the aircraft and he left the ferry pilot behind (who Ledingham believes might well actually have saved the day had he been on board, as he was an experienced Canadian bush pilot who told Ledingham later that he couldn't believe that they went up into the cloud when it was clear below). So they flew on, having turfed out all the survival equipment in the aircraft when Smith apparently decided it wasn't necessary.

Ledingham: 'So they ended up with two double sleeping bags, taken by, "Bugs" McKeith and Dave Rinning. I had, according to my diary, advised two of them to bring double sleeping bags so they had two for six people.'

****

CHAPTER SEVEN

'Twotter' Down – But Where?

Rod Ledingham and John Ayers were on the radio in the Fossil Bluff hut trying to keep track of what was going on and offering weather information.

'They flew around, and at 12.30 pm they decided they ought to go back because they'd flown down towards us until they thought they were near us. They were circling round at 3000 metres in thick cloud and circling down until they finally saw mountains at 1800 metres. We said, "You must be to the east of us on the Peninsula plateau. So go back up and come across to the west" – which they did, and still said they could see the ice plateau at 1800 metres!

'We thought this was getting dodgy. All this was in thick cloud, and by this time a long time had gone by and so they went back up to 3000 metres again and decided, much to our relief, to go home. Off they went, but again they were in cloud they didn't know where they were going, and they could not locate any beacon signal from Adelaide Island.

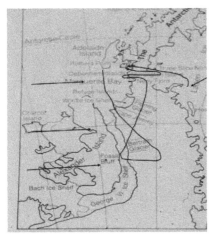

Rod Ledingham's sketched diagram trying to estimate where the Twin Otter could be.

At Fossil Bluff Rod Ledingham sent up a pilot balloon, and radioed to the Twotter that a westerly wind was blowing at 70 knots, which meant they were probably being blown over to the east if they had not corrected for the drift.

Ledingham could not work out where they were, and neither could the pilot, Squadron Leader Derek Smith. 'They must have circled around, and eventually went east – we don't know where they went.'

He surmised they must have been flying in zig-zag patterns looking for a break in the weather. Later, Ledingham concluded, they had been swept by the westerlies across the Antarctica Peninsula's high plateau, and were still there when Smith attempted to head for home, flying both east and west! After five hours flying and fuel for only 20 to 30 minutes, the aircraft was in a dire position, and Ledingham recalled Smith radioing a comment, something like, 'This is very dangerous', which under the circumstances must rate as the understatement of the year.

The pilot's only option was to land, but where? At 3000 metres they were still in thick cloud, but he set the flaps as if he were landing at that height and began to descend slowly into the murk – presumably keeping his fingers crossed that they weren't going to hit some rock-filled clouds on the way down. Mercifully he was by then over the sea ice, but that was more luck than good management.

Ledingham was listening in on the radio. His log noted tersely:

1504: report in cloud still at 6000 ft.

1522: reported at 100 ft. in sea fog but can see ice below and intend landing.

1528: reported landing and all well.

They had hit the ice at 50 metres above sea level, and come to a halt undamaged. Ledingham noted in his log:

It seems we are fated to remain at Fossil Bluff for life.

Ledingham said not very long after they landed, the weather cleared at Fossil Bluff with beautiful skies and also at Adelaide Island and Stonington over to the east.

'The Twotter party got clear weather an hour or so later. The system swept through and there was clear weather all over the Peninsula. From our experience with the Pilatus Porter we knew that the aircraft batteries would go flat very quickly so our pilot John Ayres advised them to use the radio little as possible to conserve power, and not use it for transmitting too much. Stonington also advised them to confine their answers to "yes's" and '"no's".'

'We asked them if they could see any mountains? And they said, "Yes". (One short Morse Code keystroke, known as a "dit" was no, and "dit dit" was yes.) Are they to the east of you' – we assumed they were over on the western side of the Peninsula. They said, "No". 'Are they to the north? "No". 'Are they to the south?' "Yes". What about to the west? "Yes". And somewhere to the west it was.

'So we thought, bloody hell, where the hell can they be? "Then they were asked to give one 'dit' for each 10 miles [16 km] from the mountains, dit,dit,dit,dit, dit,dit,dit,dit, eighty miles [128 km]!! Bloody hell again – we wrongly still believed they were on the western side of the Peninsula!'

Fossil Bluff Hut at the end of a long year, the Muskeg tractor parked outside. Note the dwindling supplies stacked outside the hut.

At least there was some assistance to be had from HMS *Endurance*, the new Royal Navy patrol ship, which was up in the north, around the South Orkneys at that time, en route to the Peninsula. The ship had military direction-finding gear and with all the bases on the Peninsula assisting, took part in an attempt to take bearings to pinpoint where the aircraft actually was. It was out near Cape Agazzis on the Hollick Kenyon Peninsula

'The Twotter transmitted for a minute or two. At Fossil Bluff I took the radio out onto the Sound, on to the ice, and I sat with the radio and earphones on. The others revolved the dipole aerial round me. I would yell, "Stop" when the signal blanked out and we took a bearing along the aerial. The compass bearing was passed to Stonington and the ship, and plotted.'

Eventually they pinned the aircraft down, and they were 80 nautical miles [150 km) out in the Weddell Sea on the Larsen Ice Shelf which in 1968 was 240 kilometres wide. They only had half-an-hour of fuel left when they landed. Captain Buchanan of HMS *Endurance* said he would fly fuel by helicopter over the Peninsula, which at Stonington was about 1500 metres high and 30-40 nautical miles across, where they would meet up with the Twin Otter also ready to fly the 150 km to the Weddell Sea coast with its remaining 20 minutes of fuel.

The Twotter passengers were stranded there for nine days waiting for the ship to arrive and fly the fuel in by helicopters. Pilot Derek's Smith decision to offload almost all the survival gear was unfortunate, under the circumstances. There were only two sleeping bags for six people. Ledingham:

'So they slept in shifts of three at a time for eight hours, two shifts, and they had nothing to melt water with, they had no cooker, so they actually used something which I later made sure was carried in all the aircraft survival kits when I was working with the Australian Antarctic Division – a big black plastic bag to fill with snow and put it in the window of the aircraft in the sun to melt it.

'As the emergency rations had been offloaded with other emergency gear, they lived on Dundee cake, which is a Scottish fruitcake, and fizzy drinks and stuff like that. Apparently the guy in charge, pilot Derek Smith, stepped out on to the ice and said, "Right chaps" – as he marked a spot in the snow with his heel – "This is where we'll pee, we don't want people contaminating the ice shelf". With 80 miles of ice as far as the eye could see – good idea! The golden rule applied of course — don't eat yellow snow...'

Finally the HMS *Endurance* got down to Marguerite Bay between Adelaide and Alexander Islands They were stuck north of Adelaide Island for a while but they finally got through the ice to Stonington Base. On the ninth day their helicopters flew over the plateau after seven attempts, with loads of fuel. This was very dangerous, they nearly copped trouble on the plateau around 1800 metres but they managed to sneak across with cloud moving in rapidly, got down the other side and left the fuel and sneaked back despite the weather. Icing on the rotor blades was very dangerous and so was the whiteout.

When the weather finally cleared, the Twin Otter had just enough fuel to fly unassisted to Trial Inlet on the coast where they filled up with the fuel left by the choppers and finally got back to Adelaide Island on 21 December.

They finally flew down to pick up the Fossil Bluff Five the following day.

With clear skies at Fossil Bluff an anxious watch was kept for the elusive 'Twotter'

Rod Ledingham, with camera, waiting for the longed-for rescue aircraft to arrive.

Naturally there were some please explains. Ledingham:

AT LAST! The Twin Otter lands at Fossil Bluff to complete the rescue.

'Well as soon as they picked us up from Fossil Bluff and flew us to Adelaide Island, they got orders from the Director of BAS, Sir Vivian Fuchs, to go at once to Deception Island where there had been serious volcanic eruptions. To add to this incident, the new single-engined Otter had arrived, and within days crash landed on an icefall behind Stonington and was abandoned. The passengers were picked up by the Twin Otter. No one, ordered, Sir Vivian Fuchs, was to fly anywhere until all these cock-ups had been investigated.'

'I hadn't had any mail the previous year. I'd had my last mail in December of 1966 and I had flown out down to Fossil Bluff before the mail arrived on the ship in 1967, so copped the whole lot at the end of 1968!

'Anyway I had my first bath since being stranded at Fossil Bluff when I got back to Adelaide Island, I filled the bath up and fell asleep and woke up with all this bloody mail floating in the scum and cold water all around me – my only bath in 1968. I also think I drank my two surviving bottles of beer from the two cases I had ordered from the Rose Pub in the Falkland Islands, and which had been allowed to freeze and mostly burst in an unheated store over winter!'

****

CHAPTER EIGHT

Further Adventures

After waiting eleven months for deliverance from their enforced wintering at Fossil Bluff, it was perhaps not surprising that the intrepid five's journey out of Antarctica on board the BAS research ship RRS *Shackelton* was diverted to yet another emergency.

Because the sovereignty over the Antarctic Peninsula is contested by three nations, Britain, Argentina and Chile, all three nations have their own bases scattered through the peninsula and the many islands around it. The *Shackelton* was nearing the Argentinian islands, although the British base there, Faraday, has been sold in recent years to the Ukraine and is now known as Vernadsky.

Vernadsky (a popular tourist stop now) was one of the bases in Antarctica that contributed to the discovery of the ozone hole in the upper atmosphere over Antarctica. The Ukrainians are still taking Dobson Spectrometer readings on that annual phenomenon. The British established Base F, as it was called, in 1947. Its name was changed to Faraday in 1997 to honour the British scientist Michael Faraday. However the British sold the base to the Ukraine in 1996 for the token sum of one pound. 'This', said Rod Ledingham, 'means, of course, that if you close the base in future – It's their problem. So you unload all that responsibility for a quid.'

It was while *Shackleton* was at the Argentinian islands that news of the latest violent eruption at Deception Island in February 1969 broke, and people needed to be evacuated.

Only four volcanoes in Antarctica are active, Heard Island, half way between Western Australia and the Australian Antarctic Territory, Mt Erebus on Ross Island (the scene of the terrible Air New Zealand DC7 crash in 1979), Mt Melbourne – also on the Ross Sea Coast – and Deception Island just off the northern-most tip of the Antarctic Peninsula. The latter is certainly well named. Both the major eruptions that occurred in 1967, and the most devastating in 1969, were not predicted by volcanologists.

Deception Island in winter

Deception Island was formed 10,000 years ago – a blink in geological time – and as its volcanic plug sank, it left a splendid harbor seven kilometres long by six wide, with an entrance only 250 metres wide called Neptunes Bellows. The island was much used by sealers and whalers in the late 19th and early 20th centuries. This sanctuary of course was irresistible to the three claimant nations, as safe harbours in Antarctica are rare.

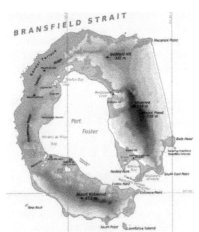

Map of Deception Island showing the caldera and sheltered harbour

By the time of the first eruption in 1967 there were three stations on Deception Island. The British Deception Island Base was just inside the entrance to the caldera in Whalers Bay, the Chilean base Pedro Aguirre Cerda was along the shore at Pendulum Cove (which was damaged and evacuated in December 1967 when there was an eruption very close to it at a place called Telefon Bay), and the Argentinians were on the south side of the bay, with their Base Decepcion, not very far away.

The Telephone Bay eruption built up an island, later called Yelcho Island, with two vents about 100 metres high, and the rock and ash falls badly damaged the Chileans' base. The Argentinians, Chileans and the British decided to leave after the 1967 eruptions, but only the British returned in December 1968 and reoccupied their base – but not for long! On the 7 February for the next three weeks they began to record ever increasing earthquakes. Ledingham:

'The second eruption in February 1969 was a massive one, it cracked the hillside for about five kilometres, and huge plumes of smoke and ash blew out. Great torrents of hot water roared down the mountainside into the caldera.

'We estimated that it could have been up to 15 metres deep, going by the tide marks on some gullies. The island is constructed like a chocolate gateau with layers of ice and ash and any eruption causes the melting of huge amounts of ice interlayered with ash and lava.'

Main vents in a huge fissure about 120 metres deep on the side of Mount Pond

The main activity was within about a kilometre of the deserted Chilean base and a chasm 120 metres deep was melted and blown out of the hillside, and as close as about 200 metres uphill from it were numerous vents and fumeroles.

The main area of activity and huge gullies formed in 1969

Ledingham: 'When the eruption went off the whole atmosphere was just filled with ash and falling rocks, lightning and thunder. The birds were flying around frantically trying to find their way through the mess. The British ran for it basically. They took a radio with them and tried to climb over to the outside of the island up over Mount Pond (700 m) to make contact with rescue vessels. The idea was to go down to the outer coast so they could get picked up by a ship – or anything!

'They alerted the British Antarctic Survey and I think the Chileans as well because they moved in with their ship and with helicopters. As the escaping Brits were on their way up this mountain the all-important radio pack was hit by a rock falling out of the sky, which smashed the radio – so that even if they had reached the outside of the island they wouldn't have been able to call anyone.

'They decided to scramble back down to their base. During that hour or two that they were away, the eruption had slackened off a bit so they raced back down to the bottom of the hill into Whalers Bay where there had been whaling factory ships and oil tanks in the early 1900s, and there were some small tin sheds still standing along the beach.

The British tried to take shelter in some small tin huts on the beach

'They got into one of these tin sheds and stayed there for a while with rocks and debris discharged into the air by the volcano, bouncing off the roof – plus lightning strikes and thunder. This went on for a while until the eruption seemed to ease somewhat and they figured there was no point in staying in this tin shed. So they kicked sheets of tin off the back of the shed, bent over the edges, and held them over their backs like Roman soldiers with their shields going into battle.'

*Desperate measures – the hut the British partly demolished to get sheets of
tin to protect their heads and backs escaping from the volcano's fury.*

The British made their way back to their base. But when they got close, they
discovered there was a huge river about 200 metres wide between them and
their base. It wasn't all that deep, and the water was warm – the ice had been
melted high on the hill behind their base, and this was running down in a huge
stream. The force of the deluge had actually moved some of the huge whaling
tanks, some 14 m high, and had washed them into the sea and repositioned
others. A lot of the whaling equipment from the shore factory and most of the
whalers' cemetery was washed completely away.

*The giant whaling tanks were picked up by the rushing waters of melted ice and
tossed about the beach like children's toys.*

When the British got back to their base, the torrent had taken out two or three rooms in the middle of the building, and left the roof suspended between the two ends. The 'Pilato Pardo" moved in close to Neptunes Bellows, the entrance to the island and their helicopters, risking very dangerous conditions with rock and volcanic ash, flew into the base in Whalers Bay just inside the entrance to Port Foster. They picked up the British staff and flew them out to the ship . With the helicopter windscreen covered covered in ash and snow some of the flying had to be done sideways, the pilots looking out of the circular side window. Brave men indeed. They were all safely landed on the ship. The *Pilato Pardo* then met up with the *Shackleton* and transferred the shaken Deception Islanders.

When Ledingham and his companions, including the evacuees, landed at the base after volcanic activity had settled, it was obvious that the flood carrying huge blocks of ice had not only taken out the booze store with all the cigarettes and so on, but the food store as well. The flood had gone right through into their living quarters which at that time was a green fibreglass hut which would have been about 20 metres long and it filled that up with ash up to the top of the roof at one end which sloped down towards where the mess and radio room were at the other.

They had had a lucky escape!

Had they not run for the outside of the island they could easily have been buried in the hut.

The hole blasted through the centre of Biscoe Hut when Rod Ledingham photographed its devastation in February 1969

Biscoe Hut and the fibreglass living quarters at the British Deception Base before the 1969 eruption

'As a result of the hasty departure all the British guys' gear was buried in their various bunkrooms. The generator was still running and a spray of ice and ash flying off the flywheel at the end of the submerged engine. The idea was to try and dig down to get their gear out. We realised this was going to be a much more difficult job than we first thought because the ash had frozen, it was like toffee. You couldn't hack it with an ice axe.'

The main volcanic activity was within about a kilometre of the deserted Chilean base and a chasm 200 metres deep was melted and blown out of the hillside, and as close as about 200 metres uphill from it were numerous vents and fumeroles. Ledingham:

The *Shackleton* was then ordered to sail to South America to pick up two volcanologists, and bring them back to Deception Island. Ledingham:

'We paused only to pick up as much plunder as we could from the debris scattered about the beaches from the block of ice that went through the middle of the hut taking out the booze and ciggy store.

'Then we had the worst crossing I've ever had anywhere on the way up to South America on the *Shackleton* when we hove-to for three days in mountainous seas off Cape Horn. Graham Smith, the geologist was sharing a cabin with me, and the water was coming in through the porthole even though we were one deck above sea level. We hadn't done a very good job of tightening the scuttle and the deadlight over the top. When we rolled, the water came down the companionway outside and jets of water came hissing in into our cabin. We didn't care because we were in the process of dying, anyway, from seasickness, and we ended up with about six inches of water on our cabin floor, sloshing back and forth.

'Around this time the cabin locker door swung open and all our sledging boxes with our goodies fell out and jammed across the doorway so nobody could get into our cabin. People were banging on the door because water was leaking into the cabins below from ours, and they were trying to get in to see what was up. By then we were in the terminal stages of seasickness where you hope the ship sinks! Graham had written a 20-odd page letter to his lady friend which was sloshing around in company with socks, shoes and lots of other debris.

'Eventually the weather settled down and we made our way north to Punta Arenas, in the Magellan Strait. When we got there, we tied up and were told we had one day ashore! We'd been away two-and-a-half years by this stage down in the Antarctic and we were allowed one day ashore, And five pounds to spend!

'We thought this was a bit tough, so at the end of the first day, one of our guys, an electrician, took a fuse out of the back of the ship's radar equipment as he knew there were no electronics people on board to realise what had happened.

'So when the Captain turned the radar on ready to sail the following morning it wasn't working. So we said, "One of our party knows how to fix it, but it'll take a while", so that was the second day we had ashore. And to fund that, we had to sell everything we could. At Deception we had found tins of tobacco and cigarettes and all sorts of stuff lying around on the beach and we found some hessian bags used for sandbags so took a whole lot of this bounty and sold it to the Chileans in Punta Arenas to fund our revelry.

'On the morning of the third day, we saw the Chilean pilot come on board to take this ship out, and before he could get to the bridge, we invited him down to our mess and plied him with gin and tonics – mostly gin. So by the time he got to the bridge he was well away, and Captain 'Frosty' Turnbull took one look at him and threw him off the bridge because he was too drunk to take the *Shackleton* through the Straits of Magellan – or anywhere. So that gave us our third day, and another sojourn on shore living the life of Riley. Apart from anything else, we hadn't seen a woman for more than two years! Well not three dimensional, only a few two dimensional ones in some Playboy magazines.'

Then it was off back to the Antarctic again to Deception Island to take the volcanologists down. When they got there, Graham Smith, the geologist, and Rod Ledingham were detailed to look after the two Cambridge volcanologists Peter Baker and John Roobol. They went ashore with them in a Zodiac each day around the volcano, landing and mapping the vents and ash falls. When they returned to the ship anchored in Whalers Bay for the night, the captain, 'Frosty' Turnbull, kept the engine running in case they had to make a run for it through the narrow entrance, called Neptune's Bellows, should another eruption start.

The vents near the Chilean base had turned it into a complete wreck since the destruction started in 1967. The heat had even melted the steel framing, and It had fallen to bits entirely.

The British base was also fairly badly damaged, but on the other side of the bay, the Argentinian base was still intact.

Peter Baker, one of the Cambridge volcanologists inspecting the new steam vents.

'We had a very interesting week and a half walking around the volcano. There was a huge crack above the Chilean base. The top half was about two hundred metres of ice, and the bottom half was about 60 metres of rock, and in the bottom of that were numerous small vents still smoking strong sulphur fumes which made you gasp for breath as the wind swirled them about. Steam was thick at times from the snow melting into the cracks in the lava. We found that we could use our ice axes to hack open the random cases of food washed up on the beach miles from the base and take the cans up to the vent and lower them into the lava where it was glowing red about 50 cm down and enjoy a hot lunch from time to time!

'We stood on the edge of the ice cliff looking down into this huge chasm which ran along the hillside for about three miles, right along nearly to the British and Chilean bases. The ground was quite unsafe with fissures and mud slides and crevasses everywhere. We nearly lost Peter Baker into a deep crack in the ash when he stepped down about two metres to stand on a snow bridge that gave way and left him hanging by the elbows surrounded by unstable ash walls. I reached down with my ice axe and he grabbed the head and hung on while the others got a rope through his rucksack straps and whisked him out.

'And nearby, on another glacier there had been an eruption there too, that had melted out the ice in the middle of it, and there was this huge circular disc that had been punched out of the glacier with vertical walls. '

'Looking down we could see streams running across under its base, and it was probably about 100 metres across from wall to wall and maybe 60 metres deep. It was quite an amazing chasm that had been melted out below by the volcano.'

Eyeing off the huge circular disk punched into a glacier – from a distance.

Up close and personal. Intrepid Rod Ledingham stands on the edge of the suddenly created chasm in the heart of the glacier.

Ledingham: 'So vast amounts of water – we estimated about 12 metres deep – had rushed down the hillside between the Chilean and British bases and washed all the ash and ice away down into the sea. Many of the blocks of ice were four or five metres long by three metres high, all scattered over the mountainside and the sand flats of the beach. It would have been one of these blocks that punched out the centre of Biscoe House.

'It was a huge eruption. It erupted again in 1971 while no one was on the island, detected by various bases on King George and Livingstone Islands, but by that time everyone had had enough sense to leave the island. The British were the last to go.

'Several visits to the island since suggest to me that the 1969 eruption was much bigger than the 1971 which was in the area of the 1967 event. Again in the same area of the caldera fault.'

Rod Ledingham and his family, wife Jeannie and daughter Kate, returned to Deception Island in 1997. They are pictured beside the forlorn carcase of the Otter which had been condemned because its tail, grafted from the wreck of another crashed Otter had come loose and was making the steering a big dodgy.

In Rod Ledingham's last exciting week there in February 1969, they only had one minor earthquake to frighten them as they were walking along the beach as far away from the ship as they could have been. Ledingham said they all started to walk faster without saying a word to each other!

'Shortly after the RRS *John Biscoe* picked us up and after a week fishing for trout in Port Stanley in the Falklands Islands we set sail for Montevideo, arriving back in Southampton to be met by my mother who had come all the way from her home in Inverness, Scotland.

'The greater part of the next seven years I spent prospecting in Western Australia and my series of lucky breaks continued. In 1971, I was overseeing a drilling program on a nickel prospect found by my boss and longtime friend Canadian Ken Thorsen, when the drill hit 140 feet of massive sulphides. This gave rise to the town of Leinster, which has just closed after 30 years of production.

'Luck again when I married Jeannie Syme and on a very hot day in the bush when we were based 100 miles north of Meekatharra in an area called Peak Hill, we spotted an advert for the Australian Antarctic Division in the paper while in Meeka getting our windscreen replaced where a 'roo had jumped through it. We applied to get away from the heat, and spent two years on Macquarie Island, followed by my working for the next 35 years mostly in the Antarctic. Jeannie, a doctor, accompanied me on more than half of her eight Antarctic trips, and daughter Kate on three before she was eighteen years old. Her first was to the Ross Sea when she was five years old. It must be addictive! They both put up with my annual absences for many years without complaining. It was probably a relief for them!

'I think I may have just done my last trip to Antarctica at 72. It's been an interesting life. I will miss it.'

****

Final Thoughts

Tim Bowden: Did you keep in touch with your Fossil Bluff party?

Rod Ledingham: Yes. The main thing I think with us lot is that we all got on well together, apart from the pilot, John Ayers, who was the odd man out. Sadly no one seems to know where he ended up, despite attempts to contact him. He spent some time flying in the Falklands, I heard. I did keep in touch with the other three, until Martyn Bramwell died suddenly some years ago. I was able to spend a couple of days with 'Brambles' in London very shortly before, in transit from Antarctica to Australia.

Graham Smith, or 'Smee' as he was called, worked for the Scottish Geological Survey and he and his wife came to Hobart a few years ago to stay with Jeannie and me and we visited him in Scotland. Since then I have made contact with him recently and he is still alive and well.

John Walsh, 'Walshie', remained in the Army and stayed with us in Cambridge nearly ten years later and we spent half the night howling with laughter at my diary of events.

Tim: Did the experience do you think change you in any way?

Rod: I can't really say. I think the only thing was I became intolerant of people who didn't know what they were doing or were lazy. You worked as a team, I guess, on both BAS bases I experienced, and there was never any real organisation of hierarchies, it was very level. We all did what was needed with very little discussion.

The way the system worked was you were chosen as an expeditioner as someone who could probably put up with life on a base and then you were trained to do something. Not like now where you have to be an expert and then they find the least insane of all the experts that apply to go. That's the way I think it's changed, everybody is an expert now, whereas in those days we were all started off as amateurs apart from our few weeks of met training.

****

Stitched-up Rod Ledingham after a year at Fossil Bluff and two years in the same clothes

Jersey patched by sewing on the legs of a pair of worn-out sea boot stockings and some leather patches from an Inuit sealskin moccasin. Trousers were stolen Argentinian pajamas, darned then patched and the patches patched with felt cut from an old mukluk boot liner.

CPSIA information can be obtained
at www.ICGtesting.com
Printed in the USA
LVHW072004211022
731269LV00017B/490